THE
WHISPERING WINGS

THIS BOOK BELONGS TO

_____

FOR THE KIDS WHO WANT TO BECOME FAIRY

ISBN: 9798894582443

IN A QUIET FAIRY GLADE, ELARA FLUTTERED HER SHIMMERING WINGS. THE WIND WHISPERED A SECRET, CALLING HER TO FIND A LONG-LOST TREASURE HIDDEN DEEP IN THE ENCHANTED FOREST.

"A TREASURE?" ELARA GASPED. HER HEART SPARKLED WITH EXCITEMENT.
SHE LISTENED CAREFULLY AS THE WIND CARRIED MYSTERIOUS WORDS, GUIDING HER TOWARD
THE ANCIENT WILLOW TREE.

ELARA FLEW PAST GLOWING MUSHROOMS AND SPARKLING STREAMS.
SHE REACHED THE OLD WILLOW TREE, ITS BRANCHES SWAYING. A TINY RIDDLE FLOATED
IN THE AIR: "FOLLOW THE MOON'S SILVER PATH."

AS NIGHT FELL, THE MOON CAST A SHIMMERING TRAIL OF LIGHT THROUGH THE FOREST. ELARA FOLLOWED, HER WINGS GLOWING SOFTLY. THE PATH LED HER TO A HIDDEN CLEARING.

IN THE CLEARING, A WISE OLD OWL HOOTED. "BRAVE FAIRY, TO FIND THE TREASURE, ANSWER THIS: WHAT SHINES BUT NEVER BURNS, MOVES BUT NEVER WALKS?"

ELARA THOUGHT HARD. "THE MOON!" SHE CRIED.
THE OWL NODDED AND POINTED TO A PATH LINED WITH TWINKLING FIREFLIES
. "FOLLOW THEM, AND YOU'LL FIND YOUR NEXT CLUE."

ELARA FLEW ALONG THE GLOWING TRAIL. THE FIREFLIES DANCED AROUND AN ANCIENT STONE, COVERED IN VINES. LETTERS WERE CARVED INTO IT, BUT THEY WERE HIDDEN BENEATH MOSS.

SHE BRUSHED AWAY THE MOSS,
REVEALING ANOTHER RIDDLE: "I SING WITHOUT A VOICE, AND DANCE WITHOUT FEET.
FIND ME NEAR RIPPLING WATERS SO SWEET."

ELARA SMILED. "A WATERFALL!" SHE FLITTED THROUGH THE TREES,
FOLLOWING THE DISTANT SOUND OF RUSHING WATER. MIST SPARKLED IN THE
MOONLIGHT AS SHE ARRIVED.

BEHIND THE WATERFALL, A GLOWING DOORWAY APPEARED.
"THIS MUST BE IT!" ELARA WHISPERED. SHE STEPPED
THROUGH AND FOUND HERSELF IN A SHIMMERING CRYSTAL
CAVERN.

GLITTERING VINES COVERED THE WALLS. IN THE CENTER STOOD A SILVER CHEST. BUT A TINY VOICE WHISPERED, "ONLY THE PURE OF HEART CAN OPEN THE FAIRY TREASURE."

ELARA CLOSED HER EYES AND THOUGHT OF ALL THE KINDNESS
SHE HAD GIVEN. SHE TOUCHED THE CHEST, AND WITH A SOFT
GLOW, IT OPENED WITH A GENTLE CLICK

INSIDE, A GOLDEN FEATHER RESTED ATOP A VELVET CUSHION. THE
WIND WHISPERED AGAIN, "THIS FEATHER HOLDS ANCIENT FAIRY
MAGIC. PROTECT IT, AND IT WILL PROTECT YOU."

ELARA HELD THE FEATHER CLOSE. IT SHIMMERED, AND SUDDENLY, SHE FELT LIGHTER, STRONGER. HER WINGS SPARKLED BRIGHTER THAN EVER BEFORE.

AS SHE STEPPED OUT OF THE CAVERN, THE WIND WHISPERED ONCE MORE. "YOUR HEART IS PURE, AND NOW, THE TREASURE'S MAGIC BELONGS TO YOU."

ELARA SMILED AS SHE FLEW HOME. THE ENCHANTED FOREST GLOWED WITH NEWFOUND LIGHT. THE FAIRY MAGIC WAS SAFE, AND SO WAS THE WONDER OF ADVENTURE.

BACK AT THE FAIRY GLADE, HER FRIENDS GATHERED. "DID YOU FIND THE TREASURE?" THEY ASKED. ELARA NODDED, HOLDING UP THE GOLDEN FEATHER.

"IT'S MORE THAN A TREASURE," ELARA SAID. "IT'S A REMINDER THAT KINDNESS, COURAGE, AND CURIOSITY ARE THE GREATEST MAGIC OF ALL."

THE FAIRIES CHEERED. THAT NIGHT, THE STARS TWINKLED BRIGHTER, AND THE WIND CARRIED ELARA'S STORY FAR AND WIDE.

AND SO,
ELARA'S ADVENTURE BECAME A LEGEND, WHISPERED THROUGH THE WIND, INSPIRING FAIRIES
FOR GENERATIONS TO COME.

ELARA PLACED THE GOLDEN FEATHER IN A SPECIAL SPOT INSIDE HER TINY HOME, WATCHING AS IT GLOWED SOFTLY, FILLING THE ROOM WITH WARMTH AND MAGIC.

AS SHE DRIFTED TO SLEEP, SHE WONDERED IF THERE WERE MORE HIDDEN TREASURES IN THE FAIRY WORLD.
PERHAPS, ANOTHER WHISPER IN THE WIND WOULD GUIDE HER.

THE NEXT MORNING, THE GLADE WAS ALIVE WITH EXCITEMENT. "TELL US MORE ABOUT YOUR ADVENTURE!" THE YOUNGEST FAIRIES BEGGED, THEIR WINGS FLUTTERING.

ELARA GATHERED THEM AROUND AND BEGAN HER TALE, DESCRIBING THE GLOWING TRAILS, THE WISE OWL, AND THE SHIMMERING CAVERN DEEP WITHIN THE FOREST

INSPIRED, THE YOUNG FAIRIES WANTED TO GO ON ADVENTURES TOO. "MAYBE ONE DAY, THE WIND WILL WHISPER YOUR NAMES," ELARA SAID WITH A WINK.

DAYS PASSED, AND ELARA FELT THE WIND AGAIN, THIS TIME WITH A NEW MESSAGE: "THE MAGIC OF THE FEATHER IS ONLY THE BEGINNING. SEEK THE FORGOTTEN STARLIGHT."

EXCITED, ELARA KNEW HER JOURNEY WASN'T OVER. SHE WOULD SOON EMBARK ON A NEW ADVENTURE —ONE FILLED WITH MORE RIDDLES, SECRETS, AND FAIRY WONDERS.

THAT EVENING, ELARA SOARED ABOVE THE TREETOPS, FEELING THE BREEZE CARRY HER HIGHER. "WHERE SHOULD I GO NEXT?" SHE WONDERED, WAITING FOR THE WIND'S NEXT WHISPER.

A SHOOTING STAR STREAKED ACROSS THE SKY. THE GOLDEN FEATHER GLOWED SOFTLY. "PERHAPS THE STARS HOLD THE NEXT SECRET," ELARA THOUGHT, HER EXCITEMENT GROWING.

DETERMINED, ELARA GATHERED A SATCHEL OF FAIRY DUST AND A TINY MAP. "A NEW JOURNEY BEGINS," SHE WHISPERED. WITH ONE LAST GLANCE AT THE GLADE, SHE FLEW TOWARD THE STARS.